BL N/A
PTS N/A

DATE DUE

KIDS' BOOK
OF
SOCCER

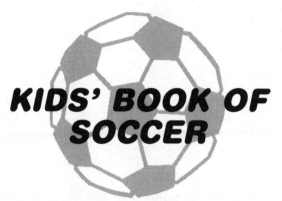

KIDS' BOOK OF SOCCER

Skills, Strategies, and the Rules of the Game

Brooks Clark

Illustrations by Tommy Stokes

A Citadel Press Book
Published by Carol Publishing Group

A Citadel Press Book
Published by Carol Publishing Group
Citadel Press is a registered trademark of Carol Communications, Inc.

Editorial, sales and distribution, and rights and permissions inquiries should be addressed to Carol Publishing Group, 120 Enterprise Avenue, Secaucus, N.J. 07094

In Canada: Canadian Manda Group, One Atlantic Avenue, Suite 105, Toronto, Ontario M6K 3E7

Carol Publishing Group books may be purchased in bulk at special discounts for sales promotion, fund-raising, or educational purposes. Special editions can be created to specifications. For details, contact Special Sales Department, 120 Enterprise Avenue, Secaucus, N.J. 07094.

Manufactured in the United States of America
10 9 8 7 6 5 4 3 2 1

Library of Congress Cataloging-in-Publication Data

Clark, Brooks.
    Kids' book of soccer : skills, strategies, and the rules of the
game / Brooks Clark.—1st Carol Pub. ed.
        p.   cm.
    "A Citadel Press book."
    Includes bibliographical references (p.   ).
    Summary: Presents information about the history, positions, and
rules of soccer and tips on basic playing techniques and strategies.
    ISBN 0-8065-1916-9 (pbk.)
    1. Soccer for children—Juvenile literature.   2. Soccer—Rules—
Juvenile literature.   [1. Soccer.]   I. Title.
GV944.2.C53   1997
796.334—dc21   97-19658
                                                                CIP
                                                                AC

Contents

Introduction

Soccer is one of the most popular games in the world. It is played by more than thirteen million boys and girls in the United States, and their numbers are growing every year. Soccer is played in 190 countries and on every continent of the world. It is one of the simplest games to play: You need only a ball, an open space, and two goals. It can be played anywhere: the front yard, the school yard, a country field. And it's fun for players at all skill levels—from beginners just learning to kick the ball to experienced pros.

In soccer, two teams compete by trying to kick the ball into the other team's goal. The main rule is that the players on the field can't touch the ball with their hands. (The only exception is the goalkeeper, or **goalie**, who can pick up the ball or knock it away to keep it from going into his own goal.) Players are allowed to touch the ball with their feet, legs, head, and chests, but not their hands, arms, or shoulders!

Soccer has been one of the world's most popular sports for more than one hundred years, and it is growing more and more popular in the United States, from youth soccer to college teams to Major League Soccer.

The *Kids' Book of Soccer* is jam-packed with tidbits about the history of the sport, useful tips on playing, and lots of interesting trivia. Whether you want to learn how to play the game better or figure out some higher-level strategies, this is the place to start.

KIDS' BOOK
OF
SOCCER

Chapter 1

A WORLD OF SOCCER

hroughout most of the world, the game of soccer is known as "football." The name "soccer" came from England, where the rules were officially laid out in 1863 by the Football Association. Players used to say they were playing under Association Rules. For short, they'd say they were playing under Assoc ("A-sock") Rules. Over time they began to say they were playing "soccer." That's the name that stuck in the United States even though the rest of the world, including the English, called it "football."

Manuscripts and drawings from ancient China indicate that in the second century B.C. the Chinese played a soccer-like game called *tsu-chu,* which means "kicking the ball with feet." The ancient Japanese played a game called *kemari,* in which teams of players kicked a ball toward a goal marked by trees.

Soccer as we know it goes back at least a thousand years in England. The modern rules were developed a little more than a hundred years ago. After the rules were made official in 1863, the game

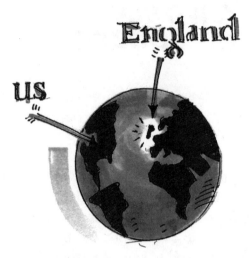

England is where it all started.

spread all over the world, helped along by the expansion of the British Empire.

In 1900, soccer was added as an event at the second Olympic Games, held in Paris. A team from England, the Upton Park Football Club, won the gold medal by defeating a French team, the Union des Sociétés Françaises des Sports Athlétiques, 4–0 in the final match.

In 1904, the Fédération Internationale de Football Associations (FIFA) was created to sponsor international competition in soccer. The first members were twelve European nations. Within a few years, they were followed by countries from South and North America, Africa, and Asia. The United States joined in 1912.

In 1930, World Cup competition began. The World Cup is an international tournament that takes place every four years, and it has been called the world's greatest single-sport event. In 1990, some 3.2 billion people watched the World Cup on TV. In 1994, 141 countries tried to be one of the twenty-four that qualified for the World Cup. That year, the World Cup was held in the United States, and for the first time, Americans got a chance to feel the excitement firsthand. The championship game between Brazil and Italy was held in the Rose Bowl in Pasadena, California, and that game alone was watched by some 2 billion TV viewers worldwide. Brazil won 3–2 in an overtime shootout!

At the 1996 Olympic Games in Atlanta, Nigeria won the Gold Medal, defeating Argentina three goals to two. This was the first time that a team from Africa had ever won a major international tournament, and the victory was one of the most exciting ever: In the semi-final game Nigeria came back from being down 3–1 to win 4–3, and in the championship game against Argentina, Nigeria came from behind twice before winning 3–2.

Today there is pro soccer in the United States, mainly in the form of Major League Soccer and two indoor leagues. There are also men's and women's college teams (see chapter 10). These teams play on a regulation field by official international rules.

If you're looking to start playing soccer, it probably comes in the shape or size that's right for you. If you're a kid playing in a local recreation league, your soccer field and your goal will be much smaller than big-time fields and goals. Instead of the usual eleven players, you may play nine to a side. If you are a kindergartener, you might play five to a side, without goalkeepers. Some teams are co-ed—boys and girls play together. There are all-boys teams, and there are also all-girls teams. There are leagues in which everybody plays an equal amount of time.

Co-ed soccer players having fun.

There are also competitive teams in which the emphasis is more on winning.

The main thing to remember about soccer is that it's fun!

It's a wonderful way to get exercise and stay fit. It's a great way to meet new friends and learn new skills. But more than anything else, it's fun to kick the ball, to dribble and pass, and to play the game!

Chapter 2

BALL + GOAL + OPEN SPACE = SOCCER

All you need to play soccer is a ball, a goal (almost anything will do), and an open space— a field, a front yard, or a corner of a playground. Let's take a look at the basic pieces of equipment.

THE BALL

A soccer ball can be made of leather, rubber, or synthetic materials. It is made up of thirty-two panels of material stitched together over a balloon-like inner liner filled with air using a pump and a needle valve.

Soccer balls are manufactured to specifications set by the controlling organization for world soccer, the Fédération Internationale de Football Associations, or FIFA, headquartered in Switzerland. The official game ball for the 1994 World Cup was the "Questra," made by the Adidas company. The balls used in many youth leagues are made in Pakistan.

A typical soccer ball.

There are five sizes of soccer balls, ranked by numbers. Sizes 1 and 2 are for souvenirs, awards, or decoration. Younger children (kindergarten through second grade) play with a Number 3 ball, which is 23.5 to 24.5 inches around and weighs 10.5 to 12 ounces. Grade schoolers use a Number 4, which measures 25 to 26 inches in circumference and weighs 11.5 to 13.5 ounces. Middle schoolers, high schoolers, college, and pro players use the Number 5, which is 27 to 28 inches around and 14 to 16 ounces. This is the "official-size" soccer ball.

THE FIELD

Soccer is played on grass or artificial turf, indoors and out. The field must always be rectangular. Official-size fields can vary between 100 and 130 yards in length and between 50 and 100 yards in width. Youth soccer fields can be much smaller, but the main parts of the soccer field are the same all over the world and for all ages!

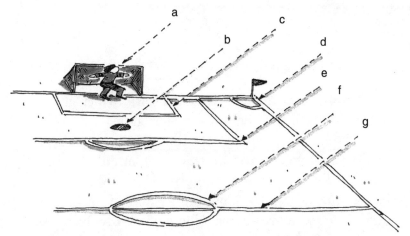

The parts of the soccer field: (a) goal; (b) penalty spot; (c) goal area; (d) corner area; (e) penalty area; (f) center circle; and (g) halfway line.

The boundary lines on either end of the field are called the **goal lines**. The lines along either side of the field are the **touch lines**. (If you're used to American football, you might call these sidelines. Don't worry: Most people will know what you mean.) All four corners of the field are marked by **corner flags**, surrounded by a quarter-circle with a radius of one yard.

This corner area is important when a defensive player kicks the ball out of bounds across his own goal line. When that happens, the offensive team gets a **corner kick**, meaning that an offensive player gets to take a free kick from the corner area toward his teammates waiting in front of the goal. Many a goal is scored off a well-aimed corner kick!

(We'll talk later about **banana kicks**, which actually curve into the goal on a corner kick!)

The line that cuts across the middle of the field is the **halfway line**. In the very middle of the halfway line is the **center spot**. This is where the ball is placed for the opening kickoff of each half and after goals are scored. The **center circle**, with a radius of ten yards, surrounds the center spot.

Unlike American football, the ball is put into play on a kickoff by the team that was just scored upon. The other team can't enter the center circle until the ball is put into play. The ball is in play after it is touched by a member of the kickoff team and travels forward at least the distance of its circumference. The player first kicking the ball cannot play it again until after it has been touched by another member of his own team.

THE GOAL

At either end of the field is a **goal**. The goal has two **posts** rising out of the ground with a **crossbar** across the top. The goalposts can be made of almost any material, including wood, metal, plastic, or fiberglass. The posts can be round, like plumbing

Goal with net backing.

pipes, square, or rectangular. Official goals should be white.

The official size for the opening of the goal is twenty-four feet wide and eight feet high. Youth goals are smaller. Tied to the crossbar and around the posts of the goal is a net, which is staked into the ground a few yards behind the goal.

The nets are important: They allow referees and players to know for sure whether a ball crossed the goal line inside or outside the goal posts or crossbar. To count as a goal, a ball must cross fully over the goal line.

WHERE THE ACTION IS

The six-yards-deep rectangular area directly in front of the goal is called the **goal area**. When a member of the attacking team kicks or heads the ball out of bounds across the goal line, a member of the defending team takes a **goal kick**, a free kick from inside the goal area (usually from the outside corner of the goal area).

The goal area is part of a larger rectangle in front of the goal, called the **penalty area**, which extends out eighteen yards in front of the goal and forty-four yards across. The penalty area is where most of the crucial action in a soccer game takes place. It is the area in which the **goalkeeper**, or **goalie**, can use his hands. It is where the attacking team makes most of its shots on goal.

It is also the area in which fouls—such as tripping, pushing, and hand balls—result in a **penalty kick**. A penalty kick is taken from the **penalty spot** twelve yards in front of the goal. Only the goalie is allowed to defend against penalty kicks, so they often result in goals!

SUITING UP

Soccer is one of the easiest sports for which to get equipped. All you need are shirts, shorts, shinguards, and a good pair of soccer shoes.

Shorts and Shirts

Soccer players wear shorts and shirts loose enough to allow quick easy movement. Lately, soccer shorts and shirts, especially made by companies like Umbro and Lanzera, have become popular as regular school attire, and why not? They look great!

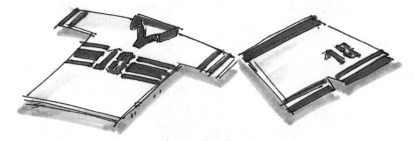

Soccer shirt and shorts.

Shinguards (inside sock).

Shinguards

Shinguards are a soccer player's best friend. They protect your shins from painful kicks. They come in all sizes, but they don't have to be huge to do the job.

Rubber cleats on a soccer shoe.

Socks

Soccer players wear long socks over their shin-guards. These come in all colors, including stripes! Soccer players always look cool in their shinguards and socks.

Cleats

Rubber-cleated soccer shoes give you traction on the grass. (If you are playing on artificial turf, you should play in regular athletic shoes.) If you take care of your cleats, they can last a long time, and you can even pass them along to a brother or sister when you outgrow them.

Do not wear your soccer shoes on asphalt or concrete: this wears down the rubber cleats! (Also, do not wear them into your house after playing a game in the mud!)

Don't track mud into the house!

Goalie Gloves and Shirts

Since goalkeepers are the only players allowed to use their hands, they must wear shirts that make them stand out from the players on both teams. For this reason, goalies often wear shirts with out-

⚽ DID YOU KNOW?

Flashy Dresser *One of the world's best and flashiest goalies,* **Jorge Campos** *of Mexico, started a fashion by wearing the flashiest most colorful shirts he could find. He kept wearing crazier and crazier shirts, and they, along with his flamboyant play far away from his goal, became his trademark. He now plays for the L.A. Galaxy of Major League Soccer.*

rageous designs and flashy colors. Goalie shirts are also made with padding in the chest and arms, for stopping or diving for balls. Keepers also wear special gloves to help them catch and hold on to balls shot at their goal.

WARMING UP

Playing soccer is a great way to stay fit because soccer players run almost the entire game. They also need strength to kick the ball and to make quick changes in direction, or "cuts," which use many different muscles. To avoid injury, soccer players must take care of their muscles. They should warm up and stretch before every practice and game. Players warm up before practices and games by:

- passing and volleying back and forth
- taking shots on the goal
- doing jumping jacks
- doing stretches

The following are basic stretches to get you started.

Hamstring

Sit on the ground with your legs stretched out in front of you. Keeping your legs slightly bent and your feet flexed (straight up and down, not pointing), gently lean over and put your face as close to your knees as you can. Hold this for 30 seconds and release. Then repeat. Don't bounce. Don't pull too hard. The best stretch is a nice, even one.

Groin Stretch

Still sitting on the ground, stretch your legs out as wide as you can and lean forward for thirty seconds and release. Then repeat.

Inner-leg Stretch

Still sitting, stretch one leg in front of you, then place the opposite foot up against your knee and lean forward again for thirty seconds and release. Then repeat.

Calf Stretch

Turn over onto all fours. Put your hands on the ground and rise up off the ground so your feet are stretching the muscles of your calves, which are the back muscles on your lower legs.

Chapter 3

PLAYING THE GAME

A soccer team is made up of eleven players. In youth leagues, this number can be ten, nine, seven, or five, depending on the age-levels of the players. A regulation soccer game is made up of two periods of forty-five minutes each. In youth soccer, the halves are shorter and divided into quarters of eight, ten, twelve, or fifteen minutes.

THE KICKOFF

The soccer game begins with a kickoff at the center spot. A player must kick it so that it rolls forward at least a ball-length. As soon as the ball rolls the distance of the ball's circumference, the opposing players can enter the center circle.

When your team kicks off, you're trying to keep control of the ball. One good kickoff play is to tap the ball to a teammate inside the center circle, who then passes out to a wing. Sometimes it's smart for that player to pass the ball back to the center midfielder, who can then decide whether to pass the ball to the outside midfielders or wings.

A proper throw-in is over the head with at
least part of each foot on the ground.

THROW-INS

The ball often goes out of bounds. When the ball goes
out of bounds along the touch lines, it is put back in
play by means of a **throw-in**. If your team last
touched the ball before it went out, the other team
gets to make the throw-in (the same as in basketball).

To make a throw-in, you can take a running
start, but you must keep both feet on the ground

until you release the ball. You must keep two hands on the ball, and your throw must come from directly behind your head. (You can't throw it like a football!)

Balls that go out of bounds over the goal lines result in two different kinds of kicks. If the attacking team kicks or heads the ball out of bounds on either side of the goal, then the defending team gets a **goal kick** from inside the goal area. If the defending team plays the ball out of bounds over their own goal line, then the attacking team gets a **corner kick**.

In certain cases, a referee will restart play with a **drop ball**. Like a face-off in hockey or a jump ball in basketball, two players stand across from each other as the referee drops the ball between them. Each one tries to gain possession of the ball.

A goal kick can be taken from anywhere in the goal area.

FOULS

Every sport has fouls, or actions that are against the rules and result in penalties. Fouls can result in two kinds of free kicks for the opposing team: a **direct kick**, which can go directly into the goal without touching another player, and an **indirect kick**, which can't go directly into the goal. To score on an indirect kick, you must pass the ball to another player, who can then try to score.

One of the most common fouls in soccer is a **hand ball**. If a player (other than the goalkeeper) touches the ball with the hands, or any part of the

Except for the goalkeeper, no one
may handle the ball in soccer.

arms up to and including the shoulder, even if it's by accident, the opposing team gets a free kick from the exact place where the foul occurred. Most of the time, this results in an indirect kick, which means that the ball has to touch another player before it can go into the goal. If a defender commits a hand ball (or any other foul, for that matter) inside the penalty area, the other team gets a penalty kick.

A penalty kick is a **direct kick**, which means that the ball can count as a goal if it goes directly into the goal without touching another player. Penalty kicks put the goalie on the spot. The keeper can move only to one side or the other—not toward the kicker—before the ball is kicked. The advantage is with the kicker, but experienced goalkeepers help the odds by remembering which side the kicker favors and jumping toward that side.

Only the goalie can defend against the penalty shot. The other defenders must stay out of the penalty area. Many games are won and lost on penalty shots, so it's important to practice them. Most penalties committed outside the penalty area result in **indirect kicks**, in which the ball must touch another player before being kicked into the goal. More serious penalties result in direct free kicks.

Tripping is a foul and will penalize your team.

It's against the rules to trip, push, or knock over another player. The best way to avoid doing all those things is to "play the ball, not the man." Sometimes players commit these fouls by accident. If the referee sees someone trip or kick another player on purpose, he or she can give that player a warning. (To do this, the ref flashes a yellow "cautionary" card.) If it happens again, the referee can eject a player from a game. (The ref does this by showing another yellow card, indicating a second cautionary offense, followed immediately by a red card.) It's also against the rules to try to make a kick above the height of your shoulders. **High kicking** is forbidden because you could kick another player in the face.

Offside

When you are on the opponent's side of the field, and the ball is passed forward to you, at the time of the pass there must be at least two defenders between yourself and the goal. If not, the referee calls your team "offside." This rule is designed to keep players from "camping" in front of the opponent's goal. In youth soccer leagues, referees begin to call teams for being offside starting in about third grade.

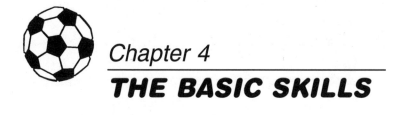

Chapter 4

THE BASIC SKILLS

DRIBBLING

Soccer players keep control of the ball as they run up and down the field by **dribbling**. Tapping the ball gently with the inside and outside of both feet, they control the ball as they run. The trick is to keep the ball close enough that no one can steal the ball but far enough that you can move quickly down the field. Good dribblers can keep the ball under control even as they stop, change direction, and make moves on their opponents.

Dribbling is a skill you can practice in your front yard or in your basement. One key to good dribbling is to keep the ball as close to your body as you can. Smart defenders watch for the moment when the ball gets a few feet in front of the dribbler, then they go in for the steal.

"Boxing"

Good dribblers are said to have a good "touch" on the ball. They can control the ball with short taps and never let it get too far away from their feet. The very best soccer players can dribble as well with one foot as they can with the other! One way to start developing this kind of touch is to dribble the ball back and forth from one foot to the other. Start off by standing with a ball between your feet. Tap the ball with the inside of one foot, then tap it back with the other. Make sure you're up on the balls of your feet so you can move with agility. Start out watching the ball as you tap it back and forth, then try to look up, as you would if you were playing soccer. Do this slowly at first, then speed up. As you improve, try to look at the ball less and look up more often.

Some soccer coaches call this "**boxing**." It's a good way to practice dribbling and to warm up. After a half-minute or so, you should begin to sweat.

Moving With the Ball

Once you're pretty good at "boxing" the ball back and forth, move the ball forward as you tap it between your feet. Then move back again. Try to look up. The better you get, the more moves you can add. For example, with the ball just outside of one of your feet, try placing your foot on top of the ball and rolling it across to the other foot. Then roll it back. This is one of the basic moves soccer players can use to get a ball by a defender, and you can teach it to yourself!

 **FUN DRILL**

"One on One" *One of the best ways to improve your dribbling is to go one on one. Take your kid brother or sister, mark off a rectangular area, and take turns trying to dribble the ball from one side to the other, while trying to get by the other person defending. In a short period of time, you will see what works and what doesn't. You will learn to stop a good dribbler, and you will develop a few moves that you can use later on in games.*

PASSING

To move the ball up the field, teammates pass the ball to each other. When you're first starting out in soccer, the basic, short pass is the **flat kick**, made with the inside of your foot. This is also called a **push pass**.

This is different from the way you kick when you're shooting on the goal and trying to score. When you're trying to get the ball by a goalkeeper, you try to kick as hard as you can, usually using the instep of your foot—just to the sides and on top of your toes. When you pass to a teammate, you want your kick to be a) accurate, and b) gentle enough that your teammate can **trap** it—that is, to control it with his or her feet.

Passing the ball upfield.

Passing with the side of your foot makes your passes more accurate and easier for your teammates to trap. Passes should be made in a quick, short motion. You can practice passing a soccer ball the same way you play catch with a baseball. Passing and trapping—like throwing and catching a baseball or a football—is definitely a skill that improves with practice!

Your soccer coach will invent many drills and fun practice games to help you and your teammates improve your passing, trapping, and ball handling. These are the skills that allow young soccer players to work together as a team and bring the ball upfield toward the opponent's goal.

You can make longer passes using the instep kick. But even your long passes should always be

A flat kick is made with the
inside of the foot.

accurate and low enough to the ground for your
teammate to be able to trap the ball and control it.
Sometimes in our team scrimmages, we make a rule
that our passes must go no higher than waist level.
To make sure the passes stay low, players who make
passes that go higher than waist level must run a
lap or do five push-ups. This definitely encourages
the players to make more accurate passes.

MARKING

When you **mark**, or cover, a player, you stick close
to that person so he isn't open to receive a pass.
This is especially important on throw-ins, goal kicks,
and corner kicks.

GETTING OPEN

When your teammate has the ball, you should
always try to get open for a pass. Getting open can
be as simple as running to an open area a few yards
away from your teammate.

 **FUN DRILLS**

Settling *To polish your settling skills, nothing works better than taking ball after ball from a coach, teammate, or kid brother or sister and settling it at your feet.*

Juggling *One of the ways soccer players can practice their trapping and settling skills is to "juggle" the ball—that is, to keep the ball in the air as long as possible by tapping it on the knee, thigh, forehead, chest, the side of the ankle, or the top of the foot. You can do this with a soccer ball or with a Hackey Sack. Either way, you soon learn to control a ball with a variety of moves. If you go to a soccer camp, you might see kids there who can juggle a soccer ball off their thighs for as many as one hundred times in a row!*

If a player is covering, or **marking**, you, you may have to run in one direction, then make a quick cut, or change of direction. It's also important to remember that your teammate can't pass a ball through or around an opposing player. It's your job

Trapping the ball.

to move to a spot where your teammate can pass the ball to you. If that means passing the ball backward, that's OK. The important thing is to keep possession of the ball so your team can continue to set up plays.

HINT: It's hard for teammates to know exactly who's open while they're dribbling the ball, watching for defenders, and trying to make plays. If you're open, say, "Open!" or "With you!"

⚽ DID YOU KNOW?

Master Juggler In 1988, a Kenyan named Allan Abuto Nyanjog kept a soccer ball aloft for 16 hours, 27 minutes, and 52 seconds!

TRAPPING AND SETTLING

The most basic way to trap a soccer ball is to let it hit the side of your foot. As the ball hits your foot, you draw your foot back, or "give," a little so the ball stops dead. The more you can "give," the less the ball bounces away and the more control you have.

A good soccer player can trap, or **settle**, a ball using the forehead, chest, thigh, knee, or different parts of the foot and ankle. The key is always to stop the ball by giving it a soft surface to bounce off gently and land at your feet, almost like a bunt in baseball. When you use your chest to drop a ball at your feet, you can often aim the ball downward.

SHIELDING

Once you've learned how to dribble and control the ball, it's necessary to learn to **shield the ball** from your opponents. When you shield the ball, you use

Juggling the ball off the thigh.

your body as a shield—that is, you protect the ball by keeping your body between the ball and the opposing player. This is the same skill used by dribblers in basketball and by skaters in ice hockey. As you see an opponent approach, you simply place your body in between the opponent and the ball. This gives you time to either start dribbling away from your opponent or to find an open teammate to pass to.

�+⚽ FUN DRILLS

The Kick-out Game *Here is a fun game that instantly teaches players to shield the ball. During a practice, your coach might place four cones on the field to make a square large enough to hold everyone on a team. Every player has a ball. When the game starts, each player must protect his or her own ball, but at the same time try to kick other players' balls out of the square. When your ball is kicked out of the square, you must leave the square. The winner is the last player left in the square. In no time at all, the players learn to protect the ball with their bodies while moving around the square.*

THE INSTEP KICK

One of the basic skills in soccer is the **instep kick**. You use the instep kick to make long passes, goal kicks, corner kicks, and shots on goal. It's the kick a defender will use to **clear** a ball as far as he can away from the area in front of his own goal. It's also the kick that's used in the National Football League to kick field goals.

In each situation, there are things you do differently to make the ball go in a different way. With-

You can't score goals this way!

out realizing it, many young soccer players imitate field goal kickers when they're making their shots on goal. Whoops! If you scoop your kicking foot under the ball and follow through with your foot pointing high in the air, the ball will fly high over the goal. No good! Shots on goal should be low and fast to make them hard for a goalkeeper to reach.

To make an instep kick, plant your opposite foot a few inches to the side of the ball. The farther back you place your plant foot, the higher your kick will go. The farther forward you plant the foot, the lower it will go. As you're planting your foot, bring your kicking leg as far back as you can. This is where you get your power. Make sure your body is balanced and square with the ball. Like a golfer making a swing, you bring your leg down and make contact with the ball.

Proper form for a low-trajectory instep kick.

To make the ball rise, your foot is at an angle to your body, and you kick the ball with the part of your shoe between your big toe and the laces. Follow through with your foot pointing in the direction you want the ball to go.

SHOOTING AT THE GOAL

The hardest shots to stop are hard and low. It's no good to accidentally kick a ball over the goal. To

 **SOCCER TIP**

Double Trouble *Everyone starts out dribbling and kicking better with one foot than the other. Make sure you practice with the other foot along with your dominant foot. A soccer player who can kick as well with either foot is twice as dangerous on the field!*

keep a shot low, plant your foot slightly ahead of the ball. Keep your foot pointed straight down and hit the ball with the tops of your laces. As you follow through on your kick, keep that kicking foot close to the ground and moving in the direction you want the ball to go.

For an instep kick, keep your foot pointed down and hit the ball with your laces.

HINT: To make sure they keep their shooting foot low, many soccer players use a trick. As they make their shots on goal, they try to land on their shooting foot. Try it a few times and see how it keeps your shooting foot (and the ball) from flying into the air.

USING YOUR HEAD!

The first time you see a soccer player play a ball off his or her forehead, it looks like it would hurt! The correct part of the head to use is the top of the forehead, almost at the hairline. This is the hardest part of your head, and once you learn to do it right, heading the ball doesn't hurt at all!

The Keys to Heading:

- Keep your mouth shut (so you don't bite your tongue)

- Keep your eyes looking up, and on the ball!

- Aim for just above your eyes, at the top of your forehead

- Get your upper body into the motion

- Attack the ball with the top of your forehead

To head the ball use the top of your forehead.

A Nifty Trick

Here's a four-step way for you and a partner to learn and practice the skill of heading. It can be hard for new soccer players to simply start heading balls thrown from fifteen or twenty feet away. This method starts with shorter distances and automatically builds in the proper motion.

1. One partner (the header) lies on the ground and gets ready to do sit-ups. The other partner (the tosser) stands near the first person's feet, holding the ball. As partner No. 1 starts to do a sit-

up, partner No. 2 gently tosses the ball so that it can bounce off the top of partner No. 1's forehead. Partner No. 1 gets used to keeping his or her eyes on the ball, and also gets used to putting the whole upper body into the motion. Do this ten times, then switch partners.

2.   The header gets on all fours. Once again, Partner No. 2 gently tosses the ball so that Partner No. 1 can head the ball, keeping his or her head up and using the body to pop the ball back to the tosser. Do this ten times, then switch.

3.   The header faces the tosser on his or her knees. Partner No. 2 again makes a gentle toss that can easily be headed. Partner No. 1 is now easily hitting the ball with the top of the forehead and automatically putting his or her upper body into the heading motion. Do this ten times, then switch.

4.   Both header and tosser are standing up. Now a toss from five or six feet away seems easy, and instead of simply letting the ball bounce off his or her head, the header can use his or her body to put some pop on the ball and even aim it in one direction or another. Do this ten times, then switch.

 **SOCCER TIP**

VOLLEY SHOTS

You're an attacking player in the penalty area. A ball is in the air a few feet off the ground, heading in your direction. The best play you can make is to meet that ball in the air with the tops of your shoes, the inside side of your ankle, the top of your thigh, or your forehead and **volley** it directly into a corner of the goal.

VOLLEYING

The way to develop your volleying skills is to practice, practice, and practice to improve your "touch" on the ball. The simplest drill is for a coach or team-

A volley shot off the thigh.

mate to gently toss a ball toward you in the air, and for you to then "volley" or tap the ball back.

You can start by using the inside of your ankle, then your forehead, then your thigh. Sound hard? You'll be surprised how fast you can improve!

To make the drill more interesting, divide into groups of three. One player stands in the middle, a few feet between the other two. The player in the middle volleys to one partner, then turns around and volleys to the other, then turns back, and so on.

 **FUN DRILL**

Your Best Pal *Try practicing your skills by using a simple piece of equipment called a dribble bag, or Soccer Pal. A fishnet bag holds a soccer ball. The bag is tied to a string with a handle. You can juggle, volley, head, or kick the ball and it comes right back!*

THE CORNER KICK

When you line up to make a corner kick, you have to decide on a strategy.

• If you can kick the ball far enough, you may want to kick it so that it flies high in the air and lands in front of the goal, where your teammates will be waiting to kick or head it in for a score. The best kick for this situation, if you can learn to do it, is a **banana kick**, or swerve shot, which can actually curve into the goal. It's called a banana kick because the ball makes an arc, like the shape of a banana, on its way to the goal. Another kick to use in this situation is the **chip shot**, which makes the ball fly high in the air with enough backspin that when it lands it bounces straight up in front of the goal.

- If you can't kick the ball all the way to the goal, or if the defenders are covering your players in front of the goal, you can make an instep pass to a teammate about halfway between the corner area and the goal. As quickly as possible, that person should trap the ball and pass to a teammate in front of the goal. This is called a **short corner**.

HINT: To take advantage of this situation, you may want to arrange a call ("one" or "two" will do) to let your teammates know whether you will be kicking for the goal or passing to a teammate, depending on how the defense is playing.

A pass to a teammate on a corner kick.

In higher levels of soccer, players can make their corner kicks so accurately that they can choose between aiming for the **far post** or the **near post**. Each choice poses different problems for the defense. A kick to the far post can work well if attacking players are there to kick the ball in the goal. The near post can be especially dangerous if the ball slips by a defender and ends up bouncing in front of the goal.

The Banana Kick

How do you make a soccer ball curve? The trick is where you make contact with the ball.

Imagine that the soccer ball is a globe of the world. It has a Northern Hemisphere and a Southern Hemisphere (a top half and a lower half). To make a ball rise up into the air when you kick, your instep should kick the lower half of the ball. The soccer ball also has a Western Hemisphere and an Eastern Hemisphere (a left and a right side). To make a soccer ball curve to one side, you should aim for the side **away from** the direction you want it to curve.

If you are making a banana kick, you want to kick the ball on the quarter nearest the ground and away from the goal line. It takes practice, but if you can make it work, the banana kick can be a valuable offensive weapon!

The Chip Shot

A chip shot is an instep kick that flies high in the air, drops in front of the goal, and bounces straight up in the air so that one of your teammates can kick, head, or volley it in for a goal. The key is backspin. The way to put backspin on your kick is to kick the lower part of the ball in a scooping motion, as if you were dishing out ice cream.

The Bicycle Kick

Every World Cup highlight film shows a **bicycle kick**, also known as a scissors kick. This is a dramatic volley shot in which a player lifts his feet off the ground, starts to fall backward and, as he is doing so, with his feet over his head, kicks the ball backward. The bicycle kick takes as long as any other soccer skill to master. It should be learned with the help of a) a coach and b) a mattress. A player must learn to fall without hurting himself. And then there's the matter of kicking the ball at the same time. The key to executing a bicycle kick safely is to land in a rolling motion on your back so that the energy of the fall is distributed evenly.

PUNTING

Once a goalie has fielded a ball, he or she can either throw it or punt it downfield. Except for the shape of the ball, punting a soccer ball requires exactly the same set of motions as punting a football. Here is the simplest way to learn to punt:

- Holding the ball with both hands, stretch your arms in front of you

- If you are right-footed, take a step forward with your left foot

- Keeping your right leg slightly bent, begin to swing it up

- At the same time let the ball drop to meet it

- The ball should hit the laces of your shoe about a third of the way through your swing. This will give you both distance and height in your kick. The lower the point of contact, the lower and longer the kick. The higher the point of contact, the higher and shorter the kick

- You'll get power from the swing of your leg and from the snap of your lower leg

- Make sure to kick through the ball and follow through so that your foot is high in the air

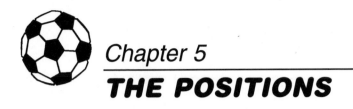

Chapter 5

THE POSITIONS

Young soccer players are often confused by the names we use for the positions in soccer, and you can't blame them. Sometimes we use different names for the exact same positions—like halfbacks and midfielders. Sometimes we talk about the three general groups of players—defenders, midfielders, and forwards. And sometimes we talk about specific positions inside the general groups. A sweeper, for example, is a specific kind of defender, and a wing is a specific kind of forward.

The fact is that terms have changed over the years. Center forwards or inside forwards are now called strikers. Fullbacks are often called marking backs. And in pro soccer, wings have all but disappeared with the sophisticated offenses being crafted for the skills of each team's forwards. Terms can differ from team to team, depending on the kind of formation. But the basic ideas remain the same.

DEFENSIVE PLAYERS—PROTECTING THE GOAL!

Defensive players have an important job: They must keep the other team from scoring a goal! Defensive players must think ahead. They must work as a team. They must know their responsibilities. They must be aggressive. They must support each other when their opponents are pushing hard toward their goal.

Are you a defender? On my teams, I like to hear my defenders growl. That tells me they have the right attitude for defending our goal!

Growling defenders!

There are many different defensive formations. The one that works for my youth soccer teams has a goalie, a sweeper, two fullbacks, and a stopper. Your team may not have a stopper, or you may not use a sweeper. What's important is that your defensive players work together and know how to stop attacking players when they come toward your goal.

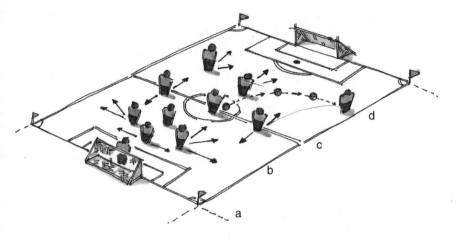

Soccer positions: (a) goalie; (b) defenders; (c) midfielders; and (d) forwards.

Goalkeeper

In big-time soccer, the goalkeeper wears the number "1" on his jersey. Some people say this is because the goalie, by keeping the opponent from scoring a goal, is often the key to victory. In World Cup competition, soccer games are often decided by a single goal, and goalkeepers who can make the great saves become national heroes. At the highest levels of soccer, the keeper is the one person on the field who cannot make a mistake. This puts a great deal of pressure on the goalie. (You might even feel the pressure when you are the goalie for your team!) Great goalies love the challenge of stopping shots on goal, and have the discipline and concentration to avoid costly mistakes in judgment. What goalies also need are good defenders in front of them!

⚽ DID YOU KNOW?

Stopping Goals   *On average, a team takes nine shots for every goal it scores. That means a keeper usually stops about eight shots out of every nine!*

Goalies wear goalie gloves to protect their hands, and the tiny suction cups in the palms help them catch fast-moving shots. Goalies also wear special shirts with protective padding sewn into the chest and arms. Many goalies like to wear knee pads, especially on artificial turf.

To play the goal, you should stand a step or two in front of your goal. You should know at all times where the ball is on the field. You must make sure your team's defensive players are ready to react to an offensive charge, and you should be ready at all times to field a ball headed toward your goal. Often, this means running out in the face of oncoming offensive players and throwing your body over the ball. Goalies must be gutsy players!

NOTE: Goalies can use their hands **only** inside the penalty area. Otherwise, a goalie could tuck the ball under an arm and run like a football player toward the opponent's goal!

Sweeper

The sweeper is the defensive player who stays in front of the keeper and tries to keep opponents from

Crazy Goalie One of soccer's greatest goalies, **Rene Higuita** of Colombia, was known to his fans as "El Loco" (the Crazy One) because he often played upfield, far outside the penalty area. He always felt he could run back into the goal in time, and most of the time he could!

---

making shots on the goal. A sweeper should have a strong leg to be able to clear balls out to the midfielders. A sweeper gives the fullbacks and stopper instructions and serves as the last line of defense before the goalie. A sweeper must be able to take on an offensive player charging toward the goal and stop his charge.

NOTE: A sweeper should always make sure his body is between the ball and the goal and never overcommit.

Fullbacks, Defenders, or Marking Backs

These are the two defensive players who play in front of the sweeper and to either side. Their job is to defend against offensive charges.

When an offensive player is dribbling a ball toward their goal, defenders run up either to take the ball away or make the offensive player pass off to a teammate. If he can, the fullback should pass the ball up to his outside midfielders so they can start an offensive charge.

If the offensive player dribbles around the fullback or successfully passes to another offensive player, the fullback should run back quickly to support the other defenders.

When your team is making an offensive charge, fullbacks can "push up" as far as midfield. In high school, college, and international soccer, fullbacks push up even farther to support offensive charges, but they have to be ready to drop back to defend! To be safe, coaches in youth soccer like their fullbacks to stay behind the midfield line.

Stopper

The **stopper** is the first line of defense. The stopper plays in front of the fullbacks and stays ready to try to stop offensive charges before they start. A good stopper catches attacking players as they cross midfield, tackles the ball and kicks it out to a midfielder to start an offensive charge in the other direction. A good stopper knows how to position his or her body between the ball and the goal. Like a good rebounder in basketball, a good stopper knows not only where the ball is, but where it's going to be. A stopper who gets a clear shot at a ball should promptly feed it to his team's outside midfielders or wings.

DEFENSIVE STRATEGY

If you look at the stopper–two fullbacks–sweeper defensive formation from above, it looks like a diamond. This formation works well in youth soccer because it protects the goal and pushes the ball toward the sidelines and upfield. The most dangerous shots on goal are made in the area directly in front of the goal. Many coaches call this area the Danger Zone, or Red Zone. Defensive players should *always* kick the ball out of their danger zone as fast as they can! This is called "taking care of business."

Tackling the Ball

In American football you tackle the man; in soccer you **tackle** the ball. One of the basic defensive moves in soccer is to charge up to an attacking player and attempt to take the ball away. To do this, a defender must keep his weight balanced on both feet, so the dribbler can't simply go around him to one side or the other. A defender must wait for the right moment and block the ball with the side of his foot.

IMPORTANT: Don't "dive in" or overcommit. If the defender makes the first move, the attacker can run around him or her on the opposite side. Wait for the attacking player to commit, then go for the tackle!

Slide Tackle

In a **slide tackle**, a defender slides his leg into the ball to steal it away from an opposing dribbler. Be careful, though: This move is allowed in regulation soccer, but for safety reasons many youth leagues forbid it.

Rules for Defenders

Here are a few rules every defender should know by heart:

- **Protect the goal.** Keep your body between the ball and the goal. It is hard to score a goal when a defender is directly in front of you

- **Kick the ball away from your goal!** When a ball is in the "red zone" in front of your goal, it is a very dangerous time. One well-aimed kick can send the ball into your goal! Defenders must act very quickly to kick balls away from the area in front of the goal. There is no time for indecision. You can kick the ball downfield or out to the sidelines. But kick it!

- **When in doubt, kick it out!** Many times in youth soccer, the smart move for a defender is to kick the ball out of bounds. Even kicking the ball over the end line and giving the other team a corner kick is sometimes a smart play. There are two main reasons: (1) you are probably surrounded by members of the opposing team, so anywhere you kick it they will get it and head toward your goal, and (2) this gives your teammates time to set up and defend

- **Deny time and space.** Get after the person with the ball as quickly as you can. Attackers love to have time to think and open spaces to move with the ball. Defenders need to take away both! Get as close to the person with the ball as you can, and don't give him or her time to think or find an open teammate. The closer you are, the less open space he or she sees. This is especially true if he or she is directly in front of the goal: The closer you are, the better chance you have of blocking the shot, or making the attacker shoot wide

- **Don't overcommit.** Charge an attacker with your weight balanced on both feet. This way you can react either way. To avoid being faked, keep your eyes on an attacker's midsection.

Watch for an opportunity to **tackle,** or take over, the ball. And avoid "diving in" with a leg. When this happens, an offensive player can simply dribble around a defender

- **Support!** Every defender gets beaten some of the time. If your teammate is taking on an attacker, position yourself behind your teammate so you're ready to take on the attacking player if he or she gets by your teammate. If you are the defender who is beaten on a play, run quickly back to help defend the goal!

MIDFIELDERS, OR HALFBACKS— CONTROLLING THE GAME

Midfielders are often the most versatile players on a soccer field. Playing between the defensive players and the forwards, **midfielders** (or **mids** for short) relay the ball upfield from the defenders to the forwards. They support offensive charges and drop back to help on defense. They are often the players who control the ball and try to set up plays. They often run from one end of the field to the other and back again in a matter of seconds!

Different teams use different numbers of

A defender moving behind a teammate to support.

midfielders. Some use two, some three, some four, or even five! Most teams use three: a right mid, a left mid, and a center mid. This is a challenging position, and it can be one of the most exciting for young soccer players.

One of the main jobs of a midfielder is to take a pass from the defender, quickly control it, and decide how to start an attacking play. If no one is on him, the midfielder can dribble upfield until a defender picks him up. Often, the best play is to pass upfield to a wing. A midfielder might also pass inside to a center forward, then quickly get open for a return pass. The key is for the midfielder to have control of the ball.

FORWARDS—GOING FOR THE GOAL!

Forwards or **strikers** are the players who line up on the front line of a soccer formation and spend the game trying to move the ball down the field, toward the opponent's goal and into the net. These are the offensive players. They make shots on the opponent's goal and do most of their team's scoring.

Wings

There are usually two wings: right and left. Their job is to play outside the other forwards, dribble the ball down the sidelines, and **cross,** or **center**, the ball to their teammates in front of the goal. Wings should be speedy in the open field. On opponent's goal kicks, wings must try to trap the ball and start another offensive play.

Striker, Center Forward, or Inside Forward

The striker is often seen as one of the most glamorous positions in soccer. The striker must be a playmaker. He must be fast and agile enough to dribble around defenders. He must be a scrappy aggressive player who can keep going when opponents are swarming around. And, most of all, he must know how to shoot and score. Like a running back in football, the center forward is a player who is at his best when it matters. The striker must see opportunities and take advantage of them.

OFFENSIVE STRATEGY

Some teams play two forwards in the middle. They might call them left striker and right striker, or left center and right center, or left inside and right inside. The job is the same. They must dribble the ball upfield and work with the other forwards to get the ball near the opponent's goal. When a wing suc-

Chipper   You scoop the ball over a line of defenders where a teammate can run and get it.

Nutmeg   If you're trying to dribble around a defender, watch for the moment when his legs are spread wide enough for the ball to pass through. Tap the ball between the defender's legs, then run around him and regain control of the ball. This move can be very embarrassing for the defender.

Swerve   You fake to one side, then go to the other.

Double Swerve   This time you go to the side you first faked to.

90   You're dribbling downfield and cut 90 degrees to one side.

180   You're running downfield and cut in the opposite direction.

270   You cut and do a three-quarter spin: Amaze your friends!

The nutmeg!

cessfully "crosses" the ball in front of an opponent's goal, the striker must close in to take a shot. When a wing sends a corner kick high across the face of the goal, the striker should be positioned and ready to tap the ball past the goalie with his head, or foot, thigh, or chest.

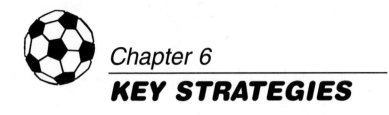

Chapter 6

KEY STRATEGIES

FORMATIONS

There is an endless variety of formations used by soccer teams, depending on the talents of the players, the coach's philosophy, and the fashion of the day. If your team lines up with three defenders, three midfielders and four forwards, that's a 3-3-4 formation. The first number refers to the defenders, the second to midfielders, and the third to forwards. So, if your team uses four defenders, three midfielders, and three forwards, that's a 4-3-3 formation. The formation most often used in pro soccer is the 4-4-2, featuring four defenders, four midfielders and two forwards. A formation growing in popularity in pro soccer is the 3-5-2, which features a sweeper and two fullbacks, five midfielders and two forwards. This formation allows pro teams to take advantage of the versatility of their midfielders, who can help attack or defend, as a situation warrants.

The fact is, those formations are only the barest framework of soccer strategy. Rather than lining up four across, a team's four defenders might be more effective lined up in a diamond, with a stopper as the first line of defense, the fullbacks as the second, and the sweeper as the final protector of the goal. On most youth soccer teams, defenders are told not to cross midfield, in case the other team makes a fast break for the goal. In higher levels of play, some defensive players push upfield almost to the opponents' penalty area to support an attack and often score goals. But they have to be able to run back quickly when the need arises.

Young soccer players have to learn that offense often comes from the outside. The defenders feed balls to the outside midfielders, who relay the passes to the wings, who dribble upfield.

Feeding a pass to the wing.

⚽ FUN DRILLS

The 2-v-1   2-v-1 is short for "two versus one," or two offensive players against one defender. This is the perfect situation for a give and go. You will probably do this drill many times in practice. You can also do it with friends at home or on the playground.

Getting Tougher: 3-v-2   Three attackers against two defenders: This is very much like what happens in game situations. The attackers must get their extra man open and get him the ball. It sounds easy, but it takes teamwork and good ball handling.

GIVE AND GO

The most basic offensive play in soccer is the **give and go**. In this play, one attacker passes (gives) the ball to an open teammate, then runs to an open area (goes) to receive a pass. This is also called a **wall pass**, since the job of the second player is to trap the ball and immediately pass it back—almost as if the ball were bouncing off a wall. Once the players on your team master the idea and the execution of the give and go, you can begin to create new plays.

Let's say your teammate has the ball. Your job is to get to a spot where he or she can pass to you.

The center gives it to the wing and then must go forward
to receive a pass.

That means getting away from a defender. The
passer is one point of a triangle, the defender is the
second, and you are the third.

TALKING TO YOUR TEAMMATES

To play well together, members of a soccer team must
communicate. You must let your teammate know if
you are open for a pass ("Open!"), or if a defender is
charging up to steal the ball away ("Man on!").

If a teammate is dribbling down the field on a
fast break, you might want to let him know you are
also running downfield and ready for a pass ("With
you!"). If you are a sweeper and the ball is in play
on the opponent's side of the field, you might direct
your fullbacks to move closer to midfield ("Push

 ## DID YOU KNOW?

Universal Language "Yo la tengo!" *It's Spanish for the call "I've got it!" Because there are so many Spanish-speaking soccer players, "Yo la tengo!" is understood around the world.*

"I've got it!" is the same in any language.

up!"). Perhaps the most basic call of all is "I've got it!" If there is a loose ball on the field, this keeps your teammates from fighting you for the ball and gives them time to get in position for a pass.

More sophisticated players can tell their teammates not only that they're open, but where they are. For example, "D left," can mean "diagonal left," telling a teammate that you are open at a forty-five-degree angle to the left of him. "Square right" tells a teammate to pass directly even with him on the right.

Chapter 7

KEEPING THE GAME GOING

THE REFEREE

The job of the referee is to make sure the game is played fairly and safely for both sides. He or she usually dresses in black. In youth soccer games, the referee will often take a moment to explain a call or a rule, so that the young players can learn the game. It is the referee's job to make sure all the players and spectators observe good sportsmanship. The referee is also the timekeeper.

A referee must use his judgment about what is a foul and what isn't. Sometimes you might hear the referee say, "Advantage," or "Advantage, play on." That's his way of telling the players that he saw the foul, but that stopping play would help the fouling team, so he has chosen to use the **advantage rule** and let play continue. (You may want to explain this rule to your parents, who sometimes get the idea that the referee isn't doing his job.)

In professional soccer, the referee carries two cards. One, a yellow card, he or she holds up to indi-

The referee holding up a yellow card.

cate that a player has been warned for committing a serious foul. The other, a red card, indicates that a player has been ejected from the game.

In soccer, there is no back-talking to the referee. If you do it once, you might get a warning. Twice, and you may give the other team a penalty kick. The referee can also expel players from the game and require a team to play with one less man!

THE LINESMEN

The linesmen stand outside the touch lines to help the referee do his job. Each linesman holds a flag. When a ball goes out of bounds, the linesman holds up the flag, pointing in the direction up- or down-field to indicate which team will get the throw-in. If there are no linesmen at your games, you may sometimes have to tell the referee which team played the ball last. It's important to be honest.

THE SOCCER COACH

Your soccer coach might be your dad or mom, or somebody else's dad or mom. It's important to listen to your coach, always have a great attitude, and remember you are a part of a team. If someone on your team hasn't learned a skill, you can try to help him or her learn it.

The soccer coach has to arrange practices and let all the parents know when to be there. Before games, he or she has to plan line-ups to make sure

DID YOU KNOW?

Mom and Dad *There are approximately 300,000 parent soccer coaches in the United States, with more signing up every day.*

everyone plays the right amount of time and that they are in positions they know how to play. If you're going to miss a practice or game, let your coach know! Sometimes he or she might plan a practice around the skills you most need to work on. It's also part of being on a team to let everyone know when you won't be able to attend.

Your coach should want you to try your best and play your hardest. The most important thing of all is that you're out there playing!

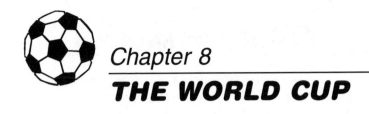

Chapter 8
THE WORLD CUP

Every four years, nations all over the world compete for the World Cup. The World Cup is soccer's world championship tournament. The first World Cup tournament was held in 1930 in Uruguay. It has been held every four years since then, except during the war years of 1942 and 1946.

In 1994, 141 nations tried to qualify for one of the twenty-two open spots in the tournament. The defending champion and the country hosting the World Cup are automatically included in the tournament, which brings the total number of teams to twenty-four. In 1994, for the first time in history, the World Cup was held in the United States.

The countries with the best soccer teams have great traditions and distinctive styles of play. Brazil is known for its exciting and artistic style of play, personified in the great **Pelé** (see page 81). It is also the only nation to have won the World Cup four times. The German team is known for being organized and disciplined and for precisely executing tactics. The Italians play with a blend of brilliant skills and hard-tackling defense. In one World Cup, Italy's defensive formation was known as *catenaccio,*

DID YOU KNOW?

Mini-country *The smallest country with a World Cup team is San Marino, the European nation of 38 square miles and with a population of 20,000.*

or "great big chain." It was made up of four defenders plus a *libero,* or a "free man," behind them. This is the position we now call a sweeper.

Argentina plays a tough and highly skilled game that makes them a special favorite of fans around the world. The greatest Argentinean star was **Diego Maradona**, one of the greatest soccer players of all time, who went on to play in Italy and is now near the end of his career. Americans, who are still catching up to the technical skills of other countries, are known for the hustle of their players such as **Cobi Jones** and **Alexi Lalas**.

WORLD CUP WINNERS

1930	Uruguay	1974	West Germany
1934	Italy	1978	Argentina
1938	Italy	1982	Italy
1950	Uruguay	1986	Argentina
1954	West Germany	1990	West Germany
1958	Brazil	1994	Brazil
1962	Brazil	1998	Likely contenders:
1966	England		Nigeria,
1970	Brazil		Argentina, Brazil

⚽ DID YOU KNOW?

"The Soccer War"   In 1969, the South American nation of El Salvador defeated its neighbor, Honduras, in a qualifying game for the 1970 World Cup tournament. Emotions ran so high that this game touched off a two-week border war and extensive riots in which, tragically, 2,000 people were killed.

THE MOST FAMOUS SOCCER PLAYER

One of the most celebrated athletes and certainly the greatest goal-scorer of all time was Edson Arantes do Nascimento, known to the world as Pelé.

He got the nickname as a young boy, when he first started playing soccer around his neighborhood. Pelé himself doesn't know what the name means. It could be short for the Portuguese word *pelada*, the kind of small, bare field Pelé played on as a child. Or it could have come from Quele, the name of one of Pelé's soccer idols.

Wherever it came from, the name Pelé is known and loved all over the world. He may be the only athlete who ever stopped a war: During a civil war in Nigeria in the seventies, a forty-eight-hour cease-fire was declared to allow soldiers and rebels to attend a Pelé exhibition.

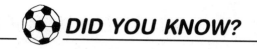 **DID YOU KNOW?**

The World's Largest Soccer Stadium
Maracanã in Rio de Janeiro, Brazil, holds more than 200,000 spectators. At one soccer game in 1950, it held 203,849 soccer fans for a World Cup final game against Uruguay. (Uruguay won 2–1.) The largest soccer stadium in the United States is the Rose Bowl in Pasadena, California, with a capacity of 105,000.

Pelé started playing for Brazil in 1958 when he was just sixteen. When he received offers to play in Europe, the Congress of Brazil declared him an official national treasure and made it illegal for him to play for another country. He retired from Brazil in 1974, then came to the United States in 1975 to play for the New York Cosmos of the North American Soccer League. While the league lasted, Pelé helped it draw huge crowds and introduce many Americans to world soccer.

In his long career, Pelé scored an unbelievable 1,281 goals, second on the all-time list to his Brazilian countryman Arthur "The Tiger" Friedereich's 1,329, which he scored between 1912 and 1937. Only one other person, Franz Binder of Austria, has ever scored more than 1,000.

Edson Arantes do Nascimento, also known as Pelé,
(AP/Wide World Photos).

Chapter 9
THE OLYMPICS

Soccer has been a part of the Olympics since the second modern Olympiad, held in 1900 in Paris. In the 1996 Games, held in Atlanta, Nigeria came from behind to beat Argentina 3–2 to become the first African nation ever to win a major international tournament. The Nigerian team was led by a 20-year-old player named Nwankwo Kanu. Tragically, medical tests done after the Olympics revealed that Kanu suffered from a serious valve disorder of the heart, and his doctors told him he could never play soccer again. The U.S. men's team, led by forward A. J. Wood and defender Alexi Lalas, went 1-1-1 in Olympic competition.

OLYMPIC MEDAL WINNERS

Year	Gold	Silver	Bronze
1900	England	France	Belgium
1904	Canada	USA I	USA II*
1906	Denmark	Smyrna**	Greece
1908	England	Denmark	Holland
1912	England	Denmark	Holland

Year	Gold	Silver	Bronze
1916	(No Olympics due to World War I)		
1920	Belgium	Spain	Holland
1924	Uruguay	Switzerland	Sweden
1928	Uruguay	Argentina	Italy
1932	(There was no soccer at the 1932 Games)		
1936	Italy	Austria	Norway
1940–44	(No Olympics due to World War II)		
1948	Sweden	Yugoslavia	Denmark
1952	Hungary	Yugoslavia	Sweden
1956	Soviet Union	Yugoslavia	Bulgaria
1960	Yugoslavia	Denmark	Hungary
1964	Hungary	Czechoslovakia	East Germany
1968	Hungary	Bulgaria	Japan
1972	Poland	Hungary	East Germany
1976	East Germany	Poland	Soviet Union
1980	Czechoslovakia	East Germany	Soviet Union
1984	France	Brazil	Yugoslavia
1988	Soviet Union	Brazil	West Germany
1992	Spain	Poland	Ghana
1996	Nigeria	Argentina	Brazil

* (The U.S. sent two teams that year.)
** (This team was made up of players from different countries and didn't compete under the flag of any one nation.)

WOMEN

The 1996 Summer Games in Atlanta were the first Olympics to include women's soccer. Women's soccer has been taken seriously only in the last twenty years or so, and advocates of the women's game had to campaign hard with the International Olympic Committee to be included in the Atlanta Games. With the exposure gained by the excellent play of the teams from China, Norway, and the United States, women's international soccer is growing in popularity around the world.

Olympic Medal Winners

Year	Gold	Silver	Bronze
1996	USA	China	Norway

On August 1, 1996, in Athens, Georgia, the U.S. Women's team, led by forwards Mia Hamm and Michelle Akers, faced China in the final match of the Atlanta Olympic Games. There were 76,481 spectators in the stands that night—the largest paying crowd ever to watch a women's soccer game. The

U.S. Women's National Team forward Shannon MacMillan.

U.S. Women's National Team forward Tiffeny Milbrett.

U.S. team won that game 2–1, on goals scored by Shannon MacMillan and Tiffeny Milbrett, who had both played college soccer at the University of Portland, in Oregon. That victory, and the Olympic gold medal, was a great moment for U.S. soccer. Although the U.S. has never been a world power in men's soccer, it is definitely a world power in women's soccer.

Of all the great players on that gold medal-winning U.S. Women's Olympic team, none are greater than Michelle Akers and Mia Hamm.

Michelle Akers

"My dream as a little girl was to be a wide receiver for the Pittsburgh Steelers," says Michelle Akers. "I practiced Hail-Mary catches daily with my dad and brother in the backyard and at school during recess with the guys. Then one day, my first grade teacher pulled me aside and told me, 'Girls don't play football.' I was crushed." Fortunately, says Michelle, with the encouragement and support of her parents, she continued in sports. She played soccer at Shorecrest High School in Seattle, Washington, at the University of Central Florida, and on the very

U.S. Women's National Team
forward Michelle Akers.

first U.S. Women's National Soccer Team, formed in 1985. Says Michelle, "We soon developed into a major international soccer power and became the first FIFA Women's World Champions in 1991. I scored ten goals in six games and was named the Golden Boot winner (highest scorer) in the tournament."

With 92 goals in 109 international matches, Michelle is the U.S. Women's National Team's all-time leading scorer. She has won many awards, including the 1988 Hermann Trophy, awarded each year to the NCAA's top male and female soccer players of the year, and the United States Olympic Committee Athlete of the Year Award in 1991. She is definitely one of the top female players in the world, but she almost didn't make it to the 1996 Olympics. In late 1993, Michelle collapsed during a soccer match and was diagnosed with Epstein-Barr virus, also known as chronic fatigue syndrome. And in 1995 she was knocked unconscious in a game and suffered a knee injury. Despite these setbacks, she fought back and helped her team win the gold medal, starting all five games of the Olympic tournament and scoring a crucial goal in the U.S. team's 2–1 semi-final victory over Norway.

Mia Hamm

With her amazing speed and lightning-quick moves, forward Mia Hamm is generally considered to be the best all-around female soccer player in the world. In her college career, she led the University of North Carolina Tar Heels to four national titles and was named to the All-America team three times. In the 1996 Atlanta Olympics, she sprained her ankle in the first round of competition, but fought through the injury to lead the U.S. Women's team to victories over Norway in the semi-finals and China in the final game. You may have seen Mia in ads on television: She was the first women's soccer player to appear in a Nike shoe ad, and later she appeared in ads for Pert Plus shampoo.

U.S. Women's National Team forward Mia Hamm.

Mia started playing soccer at the age of five. She was the youngest of four children. Her older brother and two older sisters played soccer, and her

⚽ DID YOU KNOW?

Title IX *Thanks to a United States federal law passed in 1972, girls must always have the same opportunity to play sports as boys. This has meant that many high schools and colleges now have female teams in soccer, along with many other sports. Title IX also helped the United States win Olympic gold medals in women's soccer, basketball, and softball at the 1996 Atlanta Games!*

dad was a coach, so Mia decided to play soccer, too. "At the beginning," says Mia, "I didn't like soccer more than other sports. I played so that I could be with my friends."

Mia grew up in a military family that often had to move. Her dad was a major in the air force. Whenever he was assigned to a new base, the Hamm family moved along with him. In all, Mia lived in five different states while growing up. Her last two high schools were in Wichita Falls, Texas, and Burke, Virginia.

In 1994, the University of North Carolina honored Mia by retiring Mia's college number (19). When a team retires a jersey number, it means that no other player on that team will ever wear that number.

Chapter 10

SOCCER IN THE UNITED STATES

PRO SOCCER IN THE UNITED STATES

There have been many professional soccer leagues in the United States. The most significant was the North American Soccer League, which was in existence from 1967 to 1984 and attracted such European superstars as Pelé, Franz Beckenbauer of Germany, and Giorgio Chinaglia of Italy, but in the end couldn't match football, baseball, or basketball in appealing to American fans.

There have been several semi-professional leagues since 1983, but they did not have much success. The most promising new professional league is Major League Soccer, which had its first season of play in 1996 with ten teams.

MAJOR LEAGUE SOCCER

The inaugural season for Major League Soccer came down to a championship game for the MLS Cup '96 between Washington, D.C. United and the Los

Angeles Galaxy, played on October 20, 1996, in Foxboro, Massachusetts.

Despite rain and fifty-mile-per-hour winds, 34,000 soccer fans saw a game that was tied 2–2 at the end of regulation play and won after three minutes of sudden-death overtime when D.C. United defender Eddie Pope headed in a corner kick from Bolivian midfielder Marco Etcheverry. Etcheverry, who was voted the game's Most Valuable Player, assisted on all three of D.C. United's goals!

U.S. under-23 National Team defender Eddie Pope.

Eastern Conference
Tampa Bay Mutiny
(Washington) D.C. United
New York/New Jersey
   MetroStars
Columbus (Ohio) Crew
New England Revolution

Western Conference
Los Angeles Galaxy
Dallas Burn
Kansas City Wizards
San Jose Clash
Colorado Rapids

Top Stars of the MSL

Major League Soccer has an important advantage over leagues in the past: namely, American players like Cobi Jones and Alexi Lalas, who have already earned a fan following from their years on the U.S. National Team that competed in the World Cup and in the 1992 and 1996 Olympics.

It's always easy to spot Alexi Lalas on a soccer field, with his long red hair and Vincent Van Gogh goatee. Now a 6'3", 195-pound defender with the New England Revolution, Alexi grew up mostly in Birmingham, Michigan, outside of Detroit. He learned the basics of soccer between the ages of ten and twelve, when he lived with his father in Greece. Back home, Alexi played ice hockey and soccer at the prestigious Cranbrook Kingswood High School and then at Rutgers University in New Jersey. In 1991, he won the Hermann Trophy as the NCAA's top soccer player for that year. He played on a professional team in Italy, where he learned to speak Italian, and he starred for the U.S. in the 1992 and 1996 Olympics.

Alexi is also a talented singer and guitarist. He plays in a rock band called the Gypsies, and he has released three CDs—*Woodland,* after the street he grew up on in Michigan, *Jet Lag,* and *Far From Close.* He even sang the national anthem before a soccer match in 1994.

Cobi Jones is a 5'7", 145-pound midfielder with the U.S. National Team who also led the Los Angeles Galaxy of the MLS to the league's very first championship game. Like Alexi Lalas, Cobi is easy to spot on the field, with his long braids flying up into the air as he heads a ball or moves to steal the ball from an opposing forward. Cobi is from Westlake Village, California. He played soccer and lettered in track at Westlake Village High, then played soccer at the University of California at Los Angeles (UCLA). Like Alexi, Cobi is also a media star. He hosts his own show on MTV, called *MTV Mega-dose,* and he once appeared on *Beverly Hills 90210,* playing himself.

Although they're the best known, Alexi Lalas and Cobi Jones aren't the only U.S. National Team members. As the league grows in popularity, other names will become more and more familiar to the American public. Here are some U.S. National Team players to watch for in MLS action:

- Marcelo Balboa, a 6'1", 175-pound defender with the Colorado Rapids.

- Michael Burns, a 5'9", 165-pound midfielder with the New England Revolution, played his college soccer with Hartwick College.

- Brad Friedel, a 6'4", 202-pound goalkeeper with the Columbus (Ohio) Crew, had four shutouts and eight victories in the nine games he played for Columbus in 1996.

- John Harkes, a 5'11", 165-pound midfielder with D.C. United and a native of Kearny, New Jersey, played for the University of Virginia and joined the U.S. National Team in 1987.

- Jason Kries, a 5'10" midfielder with the Dallas Burn, had thirteen goals and five assists and was ninth in the MLS in scoring in 1996.

- "Rocket" Roy Lassiter, a 5'10", 160-pound forward with the Tampa Bay Mutiny, led the MLS in scoring with twenty-seven goals and four assists in 1996.

- Brian McBride, a 6'1", 170-pound forward with the Columbus Crew, was fifth in the MLS in scoring in 1996, with seventeen goals and three assists.

- Tony Meola, a goalkeeper with the New York/New Jersey MetroStars, led the MLS with nine shutouts in 1996.

- Joe-Max Moore, a 5'9", 150-pound forward with the New England Revolution from Irvine, California and UCLA, scored eleven goals in just fourteen games in 1996.

- Eddie Pope is the D.C. United player who headed in the game-winning goal in the MLS championship game. A 6'1", 180-pound defender, Eddie grew up in High Point, North Carolina, where he played soccer and did the placekicking on the high-school football team, then went on to the University of North Carolina, the U.S. National Team, and D.C. United.

- Tab Ramos, a 5'7", 140-pound midfielder with the MetroStars, and a native of Uruguay, led his MLS team with ten assists in 1996.

- Eric Wynalda, a 6'1", 172-pound forward with the San Jose Clash, grew up in Westlake Village, California, and played youth soccer with his U.S. National teammate Cobi Jones. He is the U.S. National Team's all-time leading scorer, with twenty-seven goals.

Along with these members of the U.S. National Team, some of the most exciting players in Major League Soccer are international superstars. Here are just a few:

- Raul Diaz Arce, a forward from El Salvador, was second in the league with twenty-three goals in 1996, including four in a single game (D.C. United).

- Shaun Bartlett, a speedy forward from South Africa, had eight goals and seven assists in 1996 (Colorado Rapids).

- Jorge Campos, the veteran goalkeeper from Mexico (L.A. Galaxy).

- Mauricio Cienfuegos, a 5'6" midfielder from El Salvador (L.A. Galaxy).

- Roberto Donadoni, a midfielder from Italy (MetroStars).

- Antony De Avila, a 5'3" forward from Colombia (MetroStars).

- Marco Etcheverry, a midfielder from Bolivia, led the MLS with nineteen assists during the 1996 season. His corner kick set up Eddie Pope's game-winning goal in the championship game against the L.A. Galaxy (D.C. United).

- Eduardo Hurtado, a forward from Ecuador, scored an amazing twenty-one goals in 1996 (L.A. Galaxy).

- Preki, a midfielder from Yugoslavia, tied for second in the MLS in scoring with eighteen goals and thirteen assists in 1996 (Kansas City Wizards).

- Digital Takawira, a forward from Zimbabwe, had seventeen goals and thirteen assists in 1996 (Kansas City Wizards).

- Carlos Valderrama, a flamboyant Colombian midfielder, is the most entertaining player in the MLS. He is known for his bushy mop of curly blond hair and for his brilliant and deceptive passing. In 1996 he had seventeen assists, second best in the league (Tampa Bay Mutiny).

THE TOP COLLEGES

Soccer has been played at the college level in the United States for many years, but it has never gotten the attention of football or basketball. Between 1959, the year of the first NCAA Division I title game, and 1985, a handful of colleges dominated the soccer scene, including St. Louis Univer-

NCAA Men's Champion St. John's University forward Medufia Kulego.

sity, which has won ten championships. As soccer grows in popularity in the United States, the college game is gaining more and more fans. This is especially true of women's college soccer, which is growing because of the ever-increasing numbers of young women who want to play soccer in college, and because of the Title IX laws that are making colleges offer equal sports opportunities for females and males.

The 1996 NCAA men's championship was won by St. John's University, which defeated Florida International University 4–1 in the title game. Located in the Jamaica section of the New York City borough of Queens, St. John's has a great tradition as an NCAA basketball power, but this was the school's first national title in any sport. The final goal of the season was scored by a sophomore forward named Medufia Kulego from Malmo, Sweden. Kulego, nicknamed "K.K.," had fourteen goals and ten assists on the season, and returns in 1997 to help the Red Storm defend its title.

By far the dominant college programs in recent years have been the men's team at the University of Virginia, which has won four of the past six NCAA Division I titles, and the women's team at the University of North Carolina, which has won fourteen NCAA titles in the past sixteen years!

Much of the credit for success of the men's team at the University of Virginia goes to Bruce Arena, who coached the Cavaliers from 1978 through 1995. Coach Arena left UVA to coach the U.S. Men's Olympic team. After the Olympics, he also became coach of a Major League Soccer team, Washington D.C. United—the same team that won the MLS championship in the league's very first year of operation.

Coach Bruce Arena.

The coach at Virginia is now George Gelnovatch, who had been an assistant coach under Bruce Arena for seven years before he got the head job. In 1997, the Cavaliers will be led by Matt Chulis, a defender who has twice been named to the All-America team. He is one of three players on Virginia's team who are also on the U.S. National under-20 team.

University of Virginia men's team defender Matthew Chulis.
Chulis is a two-time All-American and is also
on the U.S. National men's under-20 team.

The University of North Carolina women's soccer program was founded in 1979 by coach Anson Dorrance. In his college days, coach Dorrance played on the UNC men's soccer team. Before that he learned how to play soccer all over the world. His father was an international businessman who traveled widely. Anson was born in Bombay, India, and grew up playing soccer in Ethiopia, Kenya, Singapore, Belgium, and Switzerland.

In 1979, when North Carolina decided to start a women's soccer team, Dorrance was named coach. In the very first season, the team won ten games and lost only two. In the second season, the team went 21–5. Since then, the Tar Heels have never lost more than two games in a season. Overall, the team's eighteen-year record is an amazing 390 wins, 16 losses and 10 ties. And don't forget those fourteen national titles!

"Obviously Anson knows what it takes to win, and that is very rare," says Olympic gold medalist Mia Hamm, who played for Carolina between 1989 and 1993. "But he makes another kind of investment in his players beyond just training: He cares about them as people. He knows what motivates certain types of players and ties it all in to team chemistry and camaraderie."

In addition to Mia Hamm, North Carolina contributed several other players to the gold medal–winning U.S. Olympic team, including midfielder Kristine Lilly, who played for the Tar Heels from 1989 to 1992, midfielder Tisha Venturini, who played

University of North Carolina team forward Robin Confer.

at UNC from 1991 to 1994, forward/midfielder Cindy
Parlow, midfielder Tiffany Roberts, and defenders
Staci Wilson, and Carla Werden Overbeck.

In 1997, one of the team's top scorers will be
Robin Confer. Robin is a right wing from Clearwa-
ter, Florida, with a knack for kicking game-win-

ning goals. Of the 57 goals she scored in her first three seasons as a Tar Heel, twenty were game-winners!

Men's NCAA Champions Since 1985

1985	University of California at Los Angeles (UCLA)
1986	Duke University
1987	Clemson University
1988	Indiana University
1989	Santa Clara and the University of Virginia
1990	UCLA
1991	University of Virginia
1992	University of Virginia
1993	University of Virginia
1994	University of Virginia
1995	University of Wisconsin
1996	St. John's University

Women's NCAA Champions Since 1985

1985	George Mason University
1986	University of North Carolina
1987	University of North Carolina
1988	University of North Carolina
1989	University of North Carolina
1990	University of North Carolina
1991	University of North Carolina

1992   University of North Carolina
1993   University of North Carolina
1994   University of North Carolina
1995   Notre Dame
1996   University of North Carolina

THE HERMANN TROPHY

Like the Heisman Trophy in football, the Hermann Trophy is presented annually to the top National Collegiate Athletic Association male and female soccer players for that year. The trophy is named after Robert Hermann, the founder of the North American Soccer League. Voting is done by college coaches and selected sportswriters.

Here are the male and female winners since 1985. (The women's trophy was first awarded in 1988.)

Year	*Men's Recipients, College*
1985	Tom Kain, Duke University
1986	John Kerr, Duke University
1987	Bruce Murray, Clemson University
1988	Ken Snow, Indiana University
1989	Tony Meola, University of Virginia
1990	Ken Snow, Indiana University

1991	Alexi Lalas, Rutgers University
1992	Brad Friedel, UCLA
1993	Claudio Reyna, University of Virginia
1994	Brian Maisonneuve, Indiana University.
1995	Mike Fisher, University of Virginia
1996	Mike Fisher, University of Virginia

Year	***Women's Recipients, College***
1988	Michelle Akers, University of Central Florida
1989	Shannon Higgins, University of North Carolina
1990	April Kater, University of Massachusetts
1991	Kristine Lilly, University of North Carolina
1992	Mia Hamm, University of North Carolina
1993	Mia Hamm, University of North Carolina
1994	Tisha Venturini, University of North Carolina
1995	Shannon MacMillan, University of Portland
1996	Cindy Daws, University of Notre Dame

Chapter 11

YOUTH SOCCER: EVERYONE CAN PLAY!

No matter whether you've already played ten seasons or none at all, there is probably a program appropriate for you. By the most recent count, 13.3 million boys and girls under the age of eighteen take part in soccer in the United States. Among kids age six to eleven, only basketball has more partipants. A **recreational league** is a good place to start. In rec leagues, everyone plays an equal number of quarters, and the emphasis is on teaching the fundamentals of the game. Most rec leagues start at age five, although the American Youth Soccer Organization (AYSO) does offer some leagues for children even younger.

Experienced players often try out for **competitive teams**. Not everyone who tries out makes a competitive team, and the emphasis is on winning games. If you try out for your middle or high school team, remember that school teams have limited numbers. Only a small number of the players who try out can make the team. Don't be discouraged: There are plenty of teams to play on.

INDOOR SOCCER

If you like playing soccer *out*doors, you might want to try playing *in*doors as well! Indoor soccer is played on a hockey-rink-sized field. The turf is artificial, so you play in sneakers instead of cleats. The "field" is surrounded by plexiglass walls, so the ball rarely goes out of play. Instead, you play the ball as it bounces off the wall. In fact, you can even make passes off the wall to your own teammates.

Like ice hockey, an indoor soccer team is made up of six players—a goalkeeper, two defenders and three forwards. Since the field is smaller, the game is faster, with an even greater emphasis on quick, accurate passes. During a season of indoor soccer, young players often find their ball-handling skills improving greatly. The play is continuous—and tiring. As in hockey, players come in and out of the game frequently, with substitutions made on the run. This makes the action extra exciting!

If you like to watch professional indoor soccer, there are two small pro leagues: the National Professional Soccer League, which has twelve teams, and the Continental Indoor Soccer League, which has seven teams and is planning to expand.

ORGANIZATIONS

AYSO

American Youth Soccer Organization (AYSO)
5402 West 138th St.
Hawthorne, CA 90250
1-800-USA-AYSO
www.soccer.org

Founded in 1964, AYSO operates soccer programs with more than 560,000 children on some 25,000 teams nationwide. The organization's success has been based on the philosophies of "everybody plays" and "balanced teams." AYSO rules require every child to play at least half of every game. The rules also require teams to be balanced every year to assure fair play. Other basic tenets of AYSO include open registration, positive coaching, and good sportsmanship.

It is AYSO's goal that young people learn to develop a positive self-image, self-confidence, and other character traits through their interest and participation in soccer. The organization depends on a nationwide network of more than 260,000 parents and friends, who serve as coaches, referees, and team administrators. A full-time staff of around forty administers AYSO from the organization's National Support Center in Hawthorne, California.

USYSA

U.S. Youth Soccer Association (USYSA)
899 Presidential Drive, Suite 117
Richardson, TX 75081
1-800-4-SOCCER

U.S. Youth Soccer Association is the official youth division of the U.S. Soccer Federation. Through fifty-five state soccer associations, U.S. Youth Soccer coordinates soccer programs for over three million players between the ages of five and nineteen, with a network of more than 250,000 coaches and 500,000 volunteers nationwide.

U.S. Youth Soccer offers both recreational and competitive programs. The recreational programs offer opportunities for players primarily interested in fun, fitness, and friendship. Small-sided games are offered for players under the age of ten. For more advanced players, USYS offers highly competitive, or "select," leagues. In addition, the USYS Olympic Development Program (ODP) identifies and develops youth players throughout the country to represent their state organizations, regions, and the United States in competitions.

The Snickers U.S. Youth Soccer National Championship, held each July, is a culmination of a year-long series of competitions at the state and regional levels for boys and girls in Under-19, U-18, U-17, and U-16 divisions. USYS also offers TOP-Soccer for young athletes with disabilities and Soccer Start for disadvantaged youngsters.

SAY

Soccer Association for Youth (SAY)
4903 Vine St.
Cincinnati, OH 45217
1-800-233-7291

Founded in 1967 by a group of volunteers interested in starting competitive recreational soccer programs, SAY has grown to include more than 73,000 children on about 6,500 teams nationally in seven age groups for boys and girls. SAY rules require every child who signs up to play at least half of each game. The objective is maximum competition with balanced competition at all age levels.

SAY's function is to provide guidance and instruction for new participants, an organizational structure to form leagues and schedule games, and to prescribe rules and regulations that will ensure safe, fair and enjoyable competition.

USSF

Unites States Soccer Federation (USSF)
1801–1811 South Prairie Ave.
Chicago, IL 60616
1-312-808-1300
socfed@aol.com

The USSF is the governing body for amateur
and professional soccer in the United States. It is
affiliated with FIFA, the international governing
body of soccer. The USYSA (see above) is the youth
division of the USSF. Another division of the USSF
is the United States Amateur Soccer Association
which governs semi-pro teams, recreational-league
teams, and city-league teams for players over nineteen years of age.

A Soccer Glossary

AYSO The American Youth Soccer Organization; founded in 1964, this organization coordinates youth leagues all over the United States. 1-800-USA-AYSO

Advantage This rule allows a referee to keep a game going after a foul if that helps the team that was fouled. When you hear a referee say, "Advantage," he's saying that he saw the foul but didn't call it because of the Advantage Rule.

Banana Kick A kick used to make the ball curve, especially on corner kicks. To make a ball curve, kick it off-center, on the side opposite the way you want it to curve.

Bicycle Kick A kick, also known as a scissors kick, that is made while falling backward with both feet off the ground, and is used by a player to kick a ball behind him. This should only be practiced with a coach.

Center *(verb)* *See* **Cross, or center**.

Chip A high arcing kick with backsping.

Clear *(verb)* To successfully kick the ball away from the front of one's own goal.

Corner Area The quarter circle, with a radius of one yard, around a corner flag.

Corner Kick The play on which the defending team last touches a ball that goes out of bounds beyond the goal line. The offensive team then kicks from the corner area toward the goal.

Cross, or center (*verb*)   To kick the ball from the side of the field toward the penalty area in front of a goal. Often the wing is the player who crosses, or centers.

Defenders   The players assigned to prevent opposing players from getting close to the goal and taking shots. These include the fullbacks, sweeper, and stopper.

Direct Kick   A free kick, awarded as the result of a foul, when a goal can be scored directly, without touching another player.

Dribble (*verb*)   To advance the ball by controlling it with your feet.

Drop Ball   A restart play in which two players stand across from one another and the referee drops the ball between them.

Forwards   The front-line attacking players, whose job is to move the ball toward the opponent's goal and score. Wings play close to the sidelines. Center forwards, or strikers, play in the middle of the field.

Free kick   A kick awarded as the result of a foul, either direct (when a goal can be scored without the ball first touching another player) or indirect (when a goal can be scored only after the ball touches another player).

Give and go   The basic offensive play in soccer, in which one player passes ("gives") to a teammate, then runs ("goes") to an open area to receive a quick pass. Also known as a "wall pass."

Goal area   The rectangular area twenty by six yards in front of the goal. Goal kicks are taken from inside this area.

Goal kick   A re-start play made by a defender from inside the goal area after a member of the attacking team last plays a ball that crosses out of bounds across a goal line. In professional soccer, goal kicks are usually taken by the goalie. In youth soccer, they are often taken by a sweeper or a fullback—whoever can kick the ball the farthest! Note: The ball is not in play until it leaves the penalty area.

Goal lines   The boundary lines along the short sides of the field, where the goals are located.

Halfbacks   *See* **Midfielders.**

Indirect kick   A free kick awarded as the result of a foul, when a goal can be scored only after the ball touches another player.

Instep Kick   A kick made with the inside front of the foot.

Juggling   Keeping the ball in the air using any legal part of the body—head, thigh, foot, chest, or knee.

Kick-off   When a team starts the play at the start of each half or after a goal has been scored.

Killing the ball   Stopping the ball by trapping it with the foot.

Marking   Guarding an opposing player to make it difficult for him to get a pass from one of his or her teammates.

Midfielders   Also known as halfbacks, these are the players who patrol the middle area of the field, between the defenders and the forwards. These players take passes from defenders and relay them upfield to their team's attackers. They support the attacks and often drop back to help on defense.

Offside   A rule, designed to prevent offensive players from "camping" in front of an opponent's goal,
which prohibits an attacking player from receiving a
pass when there are fewer than two defenders
between him and the goal.

Penalty area   The rectangular area extending eighteen yards in front of the goal in which the goalie
can use his hands. When defenders commit fouls in
this area, the offense is awarded a penalty kick
from a spot twelve yards from the goal, with only a
goalie defending.

Penalty kick   A direct free kick (that is, a kick on
which a goal can be scored without touching
another player) made from the penalty spot twelve
yards in front of the goal. Penalty kicks result from
fouls made inside the penalty area.

Penalty shoot-out   If the score of a soccer game
remains tied even after overtime periods, the teams
engage in a penalty shoot-out. The teams take turns
at taking a total of five penalty shots at the opposing goalie. The team with the most goals wins. If
they are even, the teams compete in a sudden-death
shoot-out, in which the first team to score is the
winner.

Selling a dummy   Faking the direction of a dribble
or pass to confuse a defender.

Shielding   Protecting and retaining possession of the
ball by using your body as a shield—that is, keeping
your body between the ball and your opponent.

Stopper   The defender who patrols the area in front
of the fullbacks and attempts to stop opponents'
offensive charges as they cross the midfield line.

Striker   Another name for a forward, or a player whose primary responsibility is to score goals.

Support (*verb*)   To help a defensive teammate who charges up to press an attacking player, by taking a position behind but not too close to the other defender in order to be able to pick up the attacker if he or she gets by the first defender. This is an essential part of defensive teamwork.

Sweeper   The defender who patrols the area in front of his or her own goal and behind the last line of defenders, or fullbacks.

Tackle (*verb*)   To take the ball from an opponent with a strong well-directed swing of the foot.

Throw-in   When a player sends the ball out of bounds across the touch lines, the other team is allowed a throw-in, meaning that one member of that team gets to throw the ball into play.

Touch line   The boundary line along the sides of a soccer field.

Trap (*verb*)   To gain control of a soccer ball by stopping it with your chest, feet, thigh, or head.

Volley (*verb*)   To kick the ball while it is in flight.

Wall   A line of defensive players formed in front of a goal and at least ten yards away from the spot of an opposing team's free kick.

Wall pass   A pass to a teammate that is immediately returned around the opponent. Also known as a "give and go."

Wing, or **Winger**   Name given to the right and left outside forwards.

The Seventeen Laws of Soccer

Soccer games all over the world are governed by the Seventeen Laws of Soccer. These laws are reviewed each year by the Fédération International de Football Associations (FIFA), headquartered in Zurich, Switzerland. In some years, FIFA makes small changes to the laws, but mainly these laws remain the same. Here is a summary of the official rules of soccer.

Law 1—The Field of Play

- **Dimensions.** The field is always in the shape of a rectangle. The length can be between 100 and 130 yards. The width can be 50 to 100 yards. (But the field must always be longer than it is wide.)

- **Marking.** The field is marked with lines, including the boundary lines on the longer sides of the field (the touch lines) and on the shorter sides (the goal lines). The center of the field is marked with a center spot, surrounded by the center circle with a radius of ten yards. In each corner of the field, there should be a flag on a post at least five feet high.

- **The Goal Area.** At each end of the field, two lines are drawn at right angles to the goal line, starting six yards from each goal post. These lines extend six yards into the field and are joined by a line parallel with the goal line. These lines form the goal area.

- **The Penalty Area.** At each end of the field, two lines are drawn at right angles to the goal line, starting eighteen yards from each goal post. These lines extend eighteen yards into the field and are joined by a line parallel with the goal line. These lines form the penalty area. Inside the penalty area, there is a mark made twelve yards from the mid-point of the goal line. This is the penalty mark, where all penalty shots are taken. From the penalty mark, an arc of a circle, with a radius of ten yards, shall be drawn outside the penalty area.

- **The Corner Area.** Around each corner-flag post is a quarter-circle with a radius of one yard inside the field of play.

- **The Goals.** The goals are in the center of each goal line. A goal is made of two upright posts, eight yards apart and joined by a horizontal crossbar eight feet above the ground. Goal nets can be made of hemp, jute, or nylon.

Law 2—The Ball

The official (Size 5) ball is a sphere twenty-seven to twenty-eight inches around. It should weigh between fourteen and sixteen ounces.

Law 3—Number of Players

A match is played by two teams, each made up of eleven players, one of whom is the goalkeeper. Youth league soccer games often play with fewer players.

Law 4—Players' Equipment

The basic equipment includes a jersey, shorts, socks, shinguards, and cleats. Players can't wear anything that might be dangerous to other players.

Shinguards must be covered entirely by the socks and made of a material that provides adequate protection.

The goalkeeper must wear colors that make him or her stand out from the other players and from the referee.

Law 5—Referees

The referee's job is to enforce the laws of the game. His decisions are final.

The referee can decide not to call a penalty in cases when he is satisfied that, by doing so, he would be giving an advantage to the offending team. The referee is also the official timekeeper.

If the referee sees a player commit a foul or act in an unsportsmanlike way, he can officially warn that player by showing him or her a yellow card. If a player commits another foul, or another unsportsmanlike act, the referee can officially eject a player by showing that player a second yellow card, followed immediately by a red card.

Law 6—Linesmen

The two linesmen are assistants to the referee. The linesmen tell the referee when the ball has gone out of bounds and, by means of pointing a flag in the direction of one team or the other, which team is to put the ball back in play with a throw-in, goal kick, or corner kick. They also tell the referee when a team wishes to make a substitution. The linesmen can also help the referee make calls, but the referee can always over-rule a linesman's call.

Law 7—Duration of the Game

Official soccer games are made up of two halves of 45 minutes each, with a break of 15 minutes between the halves. Youth soccer games are usually shorter and played in quarters of eight, ten, twelve, or fifteen minutes each.

Law 8—The Start of Play

Before the start of a game, the referee tosses a coin. The team that wins the toss can choose to kick off or to defend one goal or the other.

Before the kickoff, the players on both teams must be on their respective sides of the field. The players on the team not making the kickoff must remain at least ten yards from the ball until it is kicked off. At the kickoff, the ball is placed on the center spot. When the referee gives a signal, a member of the kicking team must kick the ball into the opponents' side of the field. The ball is officially kicked off after it has traveled the distance of its own circumference. The kicker is not allowed to kick the ball a second time until it has been touched or played by another player.

After a goal is scored, the team that was scored upon kicks off. After half time, the teams switch sides and the kickoff is taken by the team that didn't make the first kickoff.

Law 9—Ball In and Out of Play

The ball is out of play when it has completely crossed the goal line or touch line.

Law 10—Method of Scoring

A goal is scored when the entire ball crosses over the goal line and into the goal.

The team scoring the greater number of goals during a game shall be the winner. If no goals or an equal number of goals are scored, the game shall be termed a "draw."

Law 11—Offside

At the time the ball is passed, a player is in an offside position if he is nearer to his opponents' goal line than the ball, unless he is in his own half of the field, or is not nearer to his opponents' goal line than at least two of his opponents (usually, the last defender and the goalkeeper).

It is not considered a foul just to be in an offside position. A player is called for being in an offside position only when he or she becomes part of a play. In other words, a player can stand between the last defender and the opponent's goal, but when that player receives a pass from a teammate, he will be called for being offside.

A player can't be declared offside if he receives the ball direct from a goal kick, a corner kick, or a throw-in.

If a player is declared offside, the referee can award an indirect free kick, which is taken by a player on the opposing team from the spot where the foul occurred, unless the offense is committed by a player in his opponents' goal area, in which case the free kick shall be taken from any point within the goal area.

The offside rule is often not invoked by referees in youth soccer games.

Law 12—Fouls and Misconduct

If a player commits one of the following fouls, the referee will give the opposing team a **direct free kick**. The fouls are:

• kicking or attempting to kick an opponent

• tripping an opponent

- jumping at an opponent
- charging at an opponent in a dangerous way
- striking or attempting to strike an opponent
- pushing an opponent
- spitting at an opponent
- holding an opponent
- handling the ball (this does not apply to the goal-keeper within his own penalty area)

The direct free kick is taken by the opposing team from the place where the foul occurred, unless the foul is committed by a player in his opponents' goal area. In that case the free kick is taken from any point within the goal area.

If a player of the defending team commits one of the above ten offenses within the penalty area, he shall be penalized by a penalty kick. A penalty kick can be awarded irrespective of the position of the ball, if in play, at the time an offense within the penalty area is committed.

If a player commits any of the following fouls, the referee can award the other team an **indirect free kick**. These fouls are:

- Playing in a way considered by the referee to be dangerous (for example, attempting to kick the ball while held by the goalkeeper)

- Charging a player when the ball is not within play-ing distance of the players concerned and they are definitely not trying to play it

- When not playing the ball, running between the opponent and the ball, or using the body to form an obstacle to an opponent. (This is called "obstructing.")

- When playing as a goalkeeper, within his or her own penalty area:

  1. taking more than four steps in any direction while holding, bouncing, or throwing the ball in the air and catching it again;

  2. touching the ball with his hands after it has been deliberately kicked to him by a teammate;

  3. intentionally holding up the game or wasting time to give an unfair advantage to his own team.

A player shall be cautioned and shown the yellow card if he or she:

- persistently infringes the Laws of the Game;

- shows, by word or action, dissent from any decision given by the referee;

- is guilty of ungentlemanly or unladylike conduct.

For any of these last three offenses, in addition to the caution, an indirect free kick shall also be awarded to the opposing side from the place where the offense occurred.

A player shall be sent off the field of play and shown the red card, if, in the opinion of the referee, he or she:

- is guilty of violent conduct;

- is guilty of serious foul play;

- uses foul or abusive language;

- is guilty of a second cautionable offense after having received a caution.

Law 13—Free Kicks

Free kicks come under two headings:

- "direct," from which a goal can be scored directly against the offending side without touching another player, and

- "indirect," from which a goal cannot be scored unless the ball has been played or touched by a player other than the kicker before passing through the goal.

When a player is taking a direct or an indirect free kick inside his own penalty area, all the opposing players must stay at least ten yards from the ball and remain outside the penalty area until the ball has been kicked out of the area. The ball is in play immediately after it has traveled the distance of its own circumference and is beyond the penalty area.

When a player is taking a direct or an indirect free kick outside his own penalty area, all the opposing players must stay at least ten yards from the ball, until it is in play. The ball shall be in play when it has traveled the distance of its own circumference.

Law 14—Penalty Kick

A penalty kick shall be taken from the penalty mark and, when it is being taken, all players, with the exception of the player taking the kick and the opposing goalkeeper, shall be within the field of play but outside the penalty area, at least ten yards from the penalty mark.

The opposing goalkeeper must stand on his own goal line, between the goal posts, until the ball is kicked. The keeper can move from side to side, but cannot move toward the kicker before the ball is kicked.

The player taking the kick must kick the ball forward. He cannot play the ball a second time until it has been touched or played by another player.

A goal may be scored directly from a penalty kick.

After the player taking the penalty kick has put the ball into play, no player other than the defending goalkeeper may play or touch the ball before the kick is completed.

If the ball hits a goal post or the crossbar and rebounds into play, the player taking the penalty kick must not play it again until it has been touched by another player.

Law 15—Throw-in

When the ball goes completely over a touch line, either on the ground or in the air, it is thrown in from the point where it crossed the line, in any direction, by a player of the team opposite to that of the player who last touched it.

The thrower, at the moment of delivering the ball, must face the field of play and part of each foot must be either on the touch line or on the ground outside the touch line. The thrower must use both hands and must deliver the ball from behind and over his head. The ball is in play immediately after it enters the field of play, but the thrower cannot again play the ball until it has been touched or played by another player. A goal cannot be scored directly from a throw-in.

Law 16—Goal Kick

When the entire ball passes over the goal line (excluding that portion between the goal posts) either in the air or on the ground, having been last touched by one of the attacking team, it is kicked directly into play beyond the penalty area from any point within the goal area by a player of the defending team.

A goalkeeper cannot receive the ball into his hands from a goal kick. If the ball is not kicked beyond the penalty area, the kick shall be retaken. The kicker cannot play the ball a second time until it has touched or been played by another player. A goal cannot be scored directly from a goal kick. Players of the team opposing that of the player taking the goal kick must stay outside the penalty area until the ball has been kicked out of the penalty area.

When a goal kick has been taken and the player who has kicked the ball touches it again before it has left the penalty area, the kick must be retaken.

Law 17—Corner Kick

When the entire ball passes over the goal line (excluding the portion between the goal posts) either in the air or on the ground, having last been played by one of the defending team, a member of the attacking team shall take a corner kick, that is, the whole of the ball shall be placed within the quarter circle at the nearest corner-flag post, which must not be moved, and it shall be kicked from that position.

A goal may be scored directly from a corner kick. Players of the team opposing that of the player taking the corner kick cannot approach within ten yards of the ball until it is in play, nor can the kicker play the ball a second time until it has been touched or played by another player.

Suggested Reading

There are plenty of books about soccer, in bookstores and in the public library. You can find most of the books below in the children's section of your library.

The Great Game of Soccer by Howard Liss (1978, G.B. Putnam's Sons)

How to Play Better Soccer by C. Paul Jackson (1978, Thomas Y. Crowell)

Play the Game: Soccer by Ken Goldman & Peter Dunk (1993, Blandford)

So You Want to Be a Goalkeeper! by Joe Machnik with Paul Harris (1982)

Soccer Around the World by Dale E. Howard (1994, Children's Press, Inc.)

Soccer: From Neighborhood Play to the World Cup by Caroline Arnold (1991, Franklin Watts)

Soccer Laws Illustrated by Stanley Lover (1984, Pelham Books)

Soccer/Defense and Goal Tending by James Rothaus (1980, The Children's Book Company)

Soccer Rules: A Player's Guide by Ken Goldman (1995, Blandford)

Soccer/Team Play by James Rothaus (1980, The Children's Book Company)

Starting Soccer: A Handbook for Boys and Girls by Edward F. Dolan (1980, Harper & Row)

There are also plenty of fiction books about kids playing soccer. Here are just a few:

The Angel Park Soccer Stars Series

#1   *Kickoff Time* by Dean Hughes (1992, Bullseye Books, Alfred A. Knopf). The Angel Park kids decide to form a soccer team.

#2   *Defense* by Dean Hughes (1991, Bullseye Books, Alfred A. Knopf). Nate Matheson, goalie for the Angel Park soccer team, tries to find a way to motivate the team's defensive players.

#3   *Victory Goal* by Dean Hughes (1992, Bullseye Books, Alfred A. Knopf). Sterling Malone is a fullback who wants to be a forward, just like his brother.

#4   *Psyched!* by Dean Hughes (1992, Bullseye Books, Alfred A. Knopf). The Angel Park players are so nervous about winning their upcoming "big game" with Blue Springs that they mess up all over the place.

#5   *Backup Goalie* by Dean Hughes (1992, Bullseye Books, Alfred A. Knopf). When Nate Matheson, Angel Park's regular goalie, gets injured, he has to train Jared Trajillo to replace him.

#6   *Total Soccer* by Dean Hughes (1992, Bullseye Books, Alfred A. Knopf). The Angel Park Pride must learn to play not as a group of talented individuals, but as a single unit, if they are to win the championship.

Other Fiction

Rude Rowdy Rumors: A Brian and Pea Brain Mystery by Elizabeth Levy (1994, HarperCollins Children's Books). Seven-year-old Brian enlists the help of his little sister Penny to discover which of his soccer teammates is spreading rumors about him.

Soccer Mania by Erika Tamar (1993, A Stepping Stone Book). Nine-year-old Pete and his friends, who enjoy playing pick-up soccer, get registered as an official team and discover the negative aspects of competition.

Top Wing by Matt Christopher (1994, Little, Brown & Co.). Soccer player Dana Bellamy searches for the truth behind the fire his father is being blamed for.

The Losers Fight Back: A Wild Willie Mystery by Barbara M. Joosse, illustrated by Sue Truesdell (1994, Clarion Books). With some help from his detective partner King Kyle in Cleveland, Wild Willie and his friend Lucy figure out how to turn their soccer team into winners.